INCORRECT MERCIFUL IMPULSES

Camille Rankine

INCORRECT
MERCIFUL
IMPULSES

COPPER CANYON PRESS

Port Townsend, Washington

Copper Canyon Press is in residence at Fort Worden State Park in
Port Townsend, Washington, under the auspices of Centrum. Centrum
is a gathering place for artists and creative thinkers from around the
world, students of all ages and backgrounds, and audiences seeking
extraordinary cultural enrichment.

LIBRARY OF CONGRESS CATALOGING-IN-PUBLICATION DATA

Rankine, Camille.

[Poems. Selections]

Incorrect merciful impulses / Camille Rankine.

pages cm

ISBN 978-1-55659-490-8 (paperback)

I. Title.

PS3618.A647A6 2015

811'.6—dc23

2015024704

3 5 7 9 8 6 4 2

FIRST PRINTING

COPPER CANYON PRESS

Post Office Box 271

Port Townsend, Washington 98368

www.coppercanyonpress.org

for my parents

and their parents

Grateful acknowledgment is made to the editors of the following publications, in which these poems first appeared.

American Poet: "Failed Human Experiment," "Genealogy," "Symptoms of Aftermath"

The Atlas Review: "Syzygy," "Wake"

The Baffler: "The Free World"

Boston Review: "The Increasing Frequency of Black Swans," "Matter in Retreat," "Still Life with Spurious Picturesque," "We"

Denver Quarterly: "From the Ground," "Vespertine"

EK-PHRA-SIS: "Instructions for Modern Graffiti"

Indiana Review: "Symptoms of Sympathy"

Narrative: "Dry Harbour," "Still Life Mechanical," "Symptoms of Optimism"

Octopus: "Contact," "The Problem of Death within Life," "Symptoms of Doctrine"

Paper Darts: "Symptoms of Prophecy"

PEN Poetry Series: "The Great Dying"

Phantom: "Always Bring Flowers," "Battle Damage Assessment," "Still Life with Copernicus & Hypnophobia," "Symptoms of Prey"

A Public Space: "Dear Enemy:," "Possession"

The Recluse: "Ex Machina," "Lament for the Living"

Tin House: "The Current Isolationism," "Necessity Defense of Institutional Memory," "Tender"

Several of these poems appeared in the chapbook *Slow Dance with Trip Wire* (Poetry Society of America, 2011).

Thanks also to Easton and Olga Rankine, Jerome and Kyrra Rankine, Andrey Radovski, Hafizah Geter, Krista Manrique, Justine Post, Elizabeth Whittlesey, the MacDowell Colony, and the Cave Canem family for their support.

Contents

INCORRECT MERCIFUL IMPULSES

One

Tender

Dear patriot

Dear catastrophe

    None of this means what we thought it did

Dear bone fragments

Dear displacement

Dear broken skin

    I am in over my head

Dear prisoner

Dear, dear wounded

    You have earned our respect

Dear glad hands, curbed dog

Dear perfect object

    The same night awaits us

Dear put upon

    The day folds over and begins again

Dear bad animal

Dear caged thing

    There was something about you

Symptoms of Prophecy

In the new century,
we lose the art of many things.

For example, at the beep, I communicate
using the wrong machine.

I called to say we have two lives
and only one of them is real.

When the phone rings: you could be anybody.
In the evening: you are homeless

and hunting for good light, as safe a place
as any to make a bed for the night.

In both my lives, my nerves go bust.
I'm certain that I'm not

as I appear, that I'm a figment and
you're not really here.

The struggle
is authenticity.

I have a message.
You must believe me.

Still Life with Spurious Picturesque

The thought insists upon itself. The dead
body of it, what you have put together:

The hillside won't make sense.
You run through the trees, but the trees
lead nowhere.

Didn't the sky come down on you like.
Didn't you think you saw.

The irrational forest,
your stupid mouth,
a breath stillborn.

Define: Lake.
Ink stain. The cold, cold water.
The heart's slow beat.

There is no imagining anymore. You awake
and everything is flatter. You go outside
and there is nothing to see.

Dear Enemy:

In the city, the climate is hostile, which suits me. The people are all demand:
a sequel, a protagonist, something new to fear. Without you, we are uneasy —
what disquiet in this lack, all this emptiness to fill. Your fury is insistent, a ringing
in my ear. The hazard is high, which heightens my desire. Intelligence suggests
we were designed this way, and the city, built to keep you out, keep me in
need. The high ground is under attack, but the struggle feels far away, while that
which I desire will eventually tire me — it's more than I can bear: this interminable
want, turning and turning. The market responds favorably. Dear terror,
I come looking and I find you everywhere.

Symptoms of Island

Sometimes in the morning your hand
finds the dip in my side. For the moment

we'll call it happiness. This does not
account for weeks spent cursing

the apple trees, their sticky bloom.
The man on the bus gaping

at my slack lip knew. Plump dumb
stone in my mouth. I'm sure of it.

That afternoon you were a brisk,
starched thing. We slipped out

the back way, screen door banging
cruel on my slim-boned grim. Today,

like most days, my mind arrives
an island, tongue-numb, child wishes

ivied onto me. God takes away,
it's said. Call it what you will.

Still Life Mechanical

There is no flowering in my mind, no flower names,
no prairies, no plains, no greenery. One tree,
no leaves, two birds. No words for birds.

No fields of gold. No ripe. One hill,
no wave, no roll. I am billboards
& stone. I am all object,

all dress, no bone. No beast, no wild, no
genus, humanoid. All edifice, all lamppost,
no dusk, no star, no sky.

One half-moon, no galaxy. No mountain's majesty.
One elevator, gliding up. All pulse, dull
hum & buzz. All crave, take, thirst.

Ex Machina

Every year is the year
the world ends
as I understand it

X is to blame
or aerosol or the barbarity
of X in which we all partake

as is our way
we have come too far
to turn away from this

kernel that shapes
us into other
than animal or just

animal enough
to breed and break
it is a science

the study of what it is
in this mind and muscle
that makes us

sway the weight of us
toward give or take in the bare
face of each

open-mouthed need
and what is our mistake this clamor
that trails us that shakes us to sleep

what we are capable of
what great hope
what will become of me

Letter to the Winding-Sheet

After the snowfall, snowfall
jewels my hair, my church shoes

muddy the bedspread. *Crazy,* you
called me, *not much of a lady.*

Flip up the light switch.
A child, I act a child.

At night I hold a postcard:
two plums adorn

a plum tree, what we could be.
The door tight in its door frame,

the window keeps
shutting on me.

In every dream I dream
I am asleep, your fingers

closed around my wrists.
Your breathing steals the room.

You won't explain my shrinking
vision, why I never knew enough

about the topiary—every limb
is a root, every tree a tree.

History

Our stone wall was built by slaves and my bones, my bones
are paid for. We have two

of everything, twice heavy
in our pockets, warming
our two big hands.

This is the story, as I know it. One morning:
the ships came, as foretold, and death
pearl-handled, almost

and completely.
How cheap a date I turned out to be.

Each finger weak with the memory:
lost teeth, regret. Our ghosts
walk the shoulders of the road at night.
I get the feeling you've been lying to me.

Necessity Defense of Institutional Memory

So the free may remain free

    say the nightmare is
    the dream

so we are preserved

    he who believes takes a life

so a life may be saved

    the girl becomes an object

so the greatest devastation occurs

    let go her fingers   their slim cleave

so I may be replaced
by a machine   which in its violence   behaves
more like me

    the longer you live   the more these lies
    come alive

so the past splits in two:

    one stays in the past and dies

one past shape-shifts   walks with you.

Always Bring Flowers

Which is the way this goes again?
Lockstep with me, one-two-three,

bound in a box, taped to the floor.
Draw my next step in chalk.

Every atom of me says *faster,*
giddy up up up, skull-fractured

my skinny hope on the popcorn ceiling,
eyes full of snow.

Before we could beautify our death
it was a white noise in my head, underwater-

red. The bullet holes in the walls
were stars and stars.

I've been unrolling to a thin flat line, reaching
long for an other-side. Deliver me

from the hothouse when it's over.
Carry the first fistful of earth.

Fireblight

The Bartletts are diseased, all half-scorched
limbs and blackened leaves.
For fear of God, we avoid the dirt,

its reach. We bury the cow and we do not eat.
The television blazes through the dark.
We are living in a godless time. For fear

of dark, we try to save ourselves
and set the house on fire.
We try to save the house

and go looking for God.
Finding blood, we go looking for blood
and lose our way. *I don't want to*

set the world on fire, the car radio trills. For fear of losing,
we go looking for a fight. We break down
by the shore. *Look at how far we've come,*

the car radio tells us. *It is easy.*
Feeling easy, we lie down
in the sand and become the sand. Feeling lost,

we lie down in the sand
and become the wind, carrying ourselves away.
For fear of trial, we lose the fight.

It is easy, how the night
is beautiful. The moon bows to the earth
and is swallowed by the sea.

On the Motion of Animals

I am trying to tell you
something but my mouth
won't move

I want to hold you
but it comes all wrong
I am marooned

in this body
with no gift
for puppetry

I want to
know you I think
I could

love you like you
probably should
be loved but my love

is a fish
in the wrong
kind of water

where I want
to hold you but
there's someone else

in the room
the radiator's screaming
and my arms won't move

Symptoms of Sympathy

As it often does, all else
had failed. You wanted to fall,
but could not ignore

the landing, the truth
that the dogs had been there.
There was the question

of rain, which hung around
unanswered, a bud in your throat
refusing to bloom. The heat

was a violence that swelled
the doors and shut you out.
You said to the river, *My mind*

is a drought, what love I have
is difficult and spent.
You didn't want to hate

the living, you just wanted it to snow,
so you took this pill, held
your hand in your hand —

These are peacetime games.
The river kept running away,
coming back, running away.

Two

Still Life with Copernicus & Hypnophobia

I lose my footing   and step onto the air

     I reach for you.   It is too late for that.

Consider   Alice in her blue

     dress. Then Alice   is gone.   A coyote

baying in the fields.   It's late   and there's no one here

     to wake.   Sleep is a threat

and nothing's promised after   but an ending

     that's disheartening   for all that's left

to fathom.

        I've given up

on sense, except   the patterns

     of the morning   the way you sigh   and shield

your eyes from light.   I, too, have feared

     the sun   in its indifference   its relentless

sequence   its cause   and its effect.   This terror

     is a lesson   in mediocrity.   All I am

in the end   is a trivia, a story,

     a series of events —   my body

a collection   of particles   turning

     in space.   No place in me is worse

or better   than any place else.

Papier-Mâché and Other Human Resources

Before I learned to speak I was a bird
throat gaping, split on the first go.

I was a shower of treasures eaten
up by the floor. Despite the evidence

I've remained convinced: if the tree falls
as my voice falls, limp and unheard,

we are all done for. These thoughts will
bury me before it is time, my paper feathers

nothing if not caught backlit, pulling down
the shade, valuing our privacy.

To what degree is this imaginary: life,
imaginary hours parceled out in morsels,

each minute sifted half in one eye, half
lifted in the wind. In this way, one day

stumbles to the next, skinless and inexact.
Probably mild, probably a storm, probably

my eyes on a platter looking back.
And what do you know of war?

I would agree. I'll talk the rain, instead.
My blueing mouth. I'll swing sticks at the air.

Vespertine

Dear night: It was so warm
under you that I offered
but you refused

to endure. You won't remember
me. (We danced. I was the one
in the dark. I was wearing

this face.) In daylight, I'm an acre of empty
desert, anyway. A spent white flower. A pale
honey scent wilted away.

And I'm having this dream:
I am mourned by millions.
I died young and I was so, so pretty.

Failed Human Experiment

You are lovely the way a wall is
ten feet tall. I would believe you
blond if you told me so, boxed me
yellow in the pigment. You swore

there would be no other
apocalypse and here we are
again. It kills me
how you dig down. Mercy,

unpoison me and tell me
what for. I'm only crabgrass
green, after all,
experiencing things.

Is this my missing body,
are these your pixelated limbs,
your liquid-crystal eyes? Tell me
where the day ends, draw the line.

All night I'll watch the buildings
burn to bone from inside,
remembering: you are not mine
to be proud.

After the Fire, I Ask Myself

After the fire
I breathe standing up.

He was not a good man, but
every villain and hero loved

once — long-haired woman, white dress
billowing in the sea.

Love note penned
on the back of my hand:

Little girls prefer
pink, gentlemen.

Cowards
put their hands up.

I struck the match
on a bitter day.

Thick black drug
in a paper cup. Two cigarettes.

One for you.
One for you.

The sun really does
shine this way.

It's too cold for
my fingers, my fingers

say:
We've had enough.

Your rose-apple face.
My coal-black eyes.

Ashes.
That's why.

Symptoms of Prey

1

The night she never came back:
it stays this way.
Treat ourselves to grief.
Take my last words back.

It's funny how the day keeps.
We don't make wishes. We take our tea. Anyway,
I never knew where to put my hands
when she laughed.

2

We can only guess at these events: if the gun
came through the door first, who chased whom

in the parking lot. How much was held in
that gesture: one hand to her head, one

switching the lamp off. We know how the body
smoked after. How the blood left her like a cloud.

3

Stiff shadow of a streetlamp.

Chain link, spent match, loose brick.

Red light rolls over. Ants go about being ants.

To open your chest and put you back.

4

How does it end this way? One bite
invites another. Wound scents the water
and the sharks come. I have been flesh
hungry and at sea. I have come down
kicking. The way sweet sinks
to the bottom. That last draw.

Outliving

It's heady here under the table,
too dusty to ring the dinner bell, too heavy
to open the window and let birds

breeze in, wide and ready. Let's drink
to transients. Let's
keep the guests believing

in ghosts and we'll keep
busy waltzing, wanting
to be sliced into.

Is there anyone here
bedding the master, anyone hungry
as the night must be, lonely as Tuesday?

I've been dirigible,
changing hands, forgetting the milk.
Void and taut as a canvas ever since.

Still Life with House Finch

I used to talk to you.
In the middle of the day,

the children still
in school. What will

the pink pills do? All over
my mind there is this

empty room. Pearls tight
at my throat, pest of a bird

pecking the window.
Tell me you love me when

you find me here.
How lucky I have been.

The Problem of Death within Life

Given leave to speak, I shape my tongue
into a shovel and ask for more.
I should have told the truth, but
the truth is incomplete. I seek the missing
pieces and my eyes go lazy. It's a choice
I make that ruins me. I get off easy. I let myself go.
I hide the faces of the dying, wrap what remains
in lace and tuck it in the bottom drawer.

I'm sure I've pitied you
all wrong. I don't know how
it's done. I never learned.
I engulf with an affection from a chasm
in my gut, a sweet trapdoor, a heart-shaped hole,
a pretty well that threatens to swallow me up.

This is a brief malfunction. When you shift
out of the frame, the feeling shorts
and dissipates in sparks.
What a mess I've made of this
emotion. It's only endlessness
I've wanted. I can't fill my bowl, or yours.
I can't keep my fool mouth shut.

Symptoms of Optimism

If I've told you once, I've told you
time is a language I don't speak.

When I say *now,* I mean
mañana, chica. Was it yesterday

we were bloody-nosed, holding
our breath for the balloon to come

down, hoping for higher, higher? Maybe
freedom is a ribbon, pinning us to earth.

By nightfall, find me beginning
my descent, clinging sideways

to the ceiling. And how many days
since I've touched ground?

Morning, I'll trickle down. Tomorrow,
I promise. The birds will come.

Instructions for Modern Graffiti

Dropping bombs has lost
its thrill. The city's cleaned up and
carried you out, wiped down

its blemished memory. Done
climbing walls, you'll travel
underground. Wear an orange vest

so you don't get caught.
You won't be spared
these visions. Rats scatter. Trash fire.

Heartspray, stain the halls.
In the morning, your life
skips by, too fast

to know. You will be erased
before long: fresh paint,
an empty plate. Your eyes stung

by the natural light.
Whether or not
you exist, you did

exist. When questioned, you'll stick
to the story: alive without permission,
rusting away in the sun.

Contact

Out of respect for the departed, I still my hands, I hold
the volume of my wailing low. I gather
my spit and sweat and sorrow beneath my raincoat.
I make a blanket of all the letters
no one writes anymore. I didn't tell you
that the wind so urgent, the sound
like a wave, the dresses fluttering bright
from the storefront, my high
society, my commerce, my undimmed
night, my neon hum. Today, a near collision
with a stranger. How I tried to touch, be
known. To think a body moves me, moves
for me. To think it doesn't. To think we are alone.
Today, I feel an alien. If I could disappear.
Not a danger, not in danger. Belonging here. If I could
be the shape of your breath in the cold. What camouflage
have we. How we bury our living
within us. This precious ache I cradle, my treasure,
my dread. What barren, what beauty it makes of me.

The Current Isolationism

In the half-light, I am most
at home, my shadow
as company.

When I feel hot, I push a button
to make it stop. I mean this stain on my mind
I can't get out. How human

I seem. Like modern man,
I traffic in extinction. I have a gift.
Like an animal, I sustain.

A flock of birds
when touched, I scatter. I won't approach
until the back is turned.

My heart betrays. I confess: I am afraid.
How selfish of me.
When there's no one here, I halve

the distance between
our bodies infinitesimally.
In this long passageway, I pose

against the wallpaper, dig
my heels in, catch the light.
In my vision, the back door opens

on a garden that is always
in bloom. The dogs
are chained so they can't attack like I know

they want to. In the next yard
over, honeybees swarm
and their sound is huge.

Wilt

What is this flawed obedience?
There's only one of me, I guard my door
at noon and in the early dark
I put myself away. At dawn,
a man approaches. The man is you.
He tells me to keep going, I say
yes and we argue all day. I tell him
to forget me. I dislike this warmth, I worry
at my own fat want, a hobby.
I am not good, I do not strive
for it. I am quiet, unmerited
bleak. I am tragic and the sky
appears red. I am passionate, of course: I kneel.
I tear at the floorboards. I am dirt
and all the nights that keep ending like this:
I return from the party, my life is smoke,
I fall asleep trying to seduce you.

Wake

I turn to you to find
there is no you,
which means it's morning

and I will fail
at everything today.

The telephone will ring its brisk
and I won't answer.

A plume of gnats
will besiege my dying
bouquet.

I can stop this anytime
or I can't, I can't

decide, do I
cup my hands to receive

some element of grace, or
brace my frame against the harsh
that I create.

Through the wall the neighbors
are at play. One girl laughs

and her laugh is a disease, or a moth
at the porch light, a frenzy
of wings.

Come back.
It's cold.

The world is full of objects
that mean nothing to me.

The train sweeping its platform clean.
The window's tapestry
of past rains.

Angles of light glide across the carpet
and I gather in their shapes
until the streetlamps blink awake.

The hours move in this condition.
A terrible consonance of days.

Symptoms of Aftermath

Tonight, I dream the dead and how they want
me. They scale the walls. They tear a skylight
to the sky. I, requiring life, start a fire
and burn them all up. Lady Luck arrives late, we drive our bodies
to the dump. Afraid in the dark, I shake her
by the shoulders. *Where will the survivors congregate?*
How will we have our eggs? We ration out our breath
in the bomb shelter. Luck doesn't make it. *There was nothing*
anyone could have done. When I am saved, a slim nurse
leans out of the white light. *I need*
to hear your voice, sweetheart. I see
my escape. I walk into the water.
The sky is blue like the ocean,
which is blue like the sky.

Three

The Increasing Frequency of Black Swans

I was listening for the dog
when the locks were pried open.
The man was dead. The dog, a survivor,
was dead. It happens

more often this way.
A disease left
untreated; the body,
in confusion, gives in.

The bomb breathes its fire down
the hallway, the son comes back
in pieces; the body,
in confusion, gives in.

The grief is a planet. A dust ring.
A small moon that's been hidden
under my pillow, that's been changing
the way my body moves this whole time.

Symptoms of Doctrine

In all my stories, nothing keeps
happening over and over.
I would speak of what I know,

but what I know is nothing, except nothing
is certain. I am just trying to be
honest. Like the door and its squeak.

Is that honesty?
In all your photographs, your mouth
reminds me of my mouth, and everything

happens without me. I have been othered away
at the cusp of evening. I will find you
sleeping in the hallways. I will wake you

when the walls come loose, when my mouth
comes tumbling.
In all my photographs,

I have the same affliction.
I have been burdened
with glorious purpose.

I am trying to be certain
we are nothing
without certainty.

In all your stories, I have turned
against the wind as the wind
is cruel and won't change

course. I will pray for
the living. We are merciful.
We are just trying to be.

We are the work of a woman and a man, an effort
in breath, an indecent thing, these wars
blessed to our bodies.

In all my memories, a story
keeps being rewritten. I am just trying
to be merciful. Is that honesty?

Possession

I want to give you everything.
This is called a sickness.
By way of remedy, I am decorum
bound, swept

up and hushed. I forget myself.
I lay my goods down, lay my arms down
in the dust. Then it's a heaviness
I borrow and am taught

to own. What's mine is mine. What's ours
is the stake, the hangman's rope.
Then the cargo of dead unclaimed
that I cannot contain. I cast my doubt

upon the ground, I let
the arrows of my longing fly
toward the other shore.
I want to save you. This condition

is a viper's poison. I am bitten, my limbless
sweet sliding under the brush.
I arrived in the first world heavy
fated with this vision. I lay hold

of everything in sight.
My arms are full, the other shore
besieged by longing. I am
a sickness. I want to give you more.

Battle Damage Assessment

The man we sought wasn't
home that day. Fire stormed

through the roof—they
changed tile for cement

and prayed. In our night vision,
white was warmth, bright

body count took to the air.
The desired effect

ricocheted off the taut
firmament, the tide slid

out again. At the podium
the tone was sanguine.

The Great Dying

this is what happens: the sky
provides   the ground opens   one day

swallows a man entire   the smoke
lifts   the citizens gathering

on the hilltop   the citizens consume
the scene   a nation

cheers   a nation mourns   this
is what happens: a woman hangs

her head   a good citizen
an exhibition   a woman

moving in the wrong
body   quick

combustion   each voice armed
and at the ready   each heart

moving   just keeping on
like a muscle   what is

a country   what category of disaster
this is what happens: the sky

where we imagine
tumult just is   it is

the end   we seek
shelter   we are good

citizens   we shut up
our eyes   for so long

we wait and wait
the room grows   smaller

the sea   rises up
to meet us

From the Ground

The soldiers come down
from the forest and I warm

my hope in a bowl for you.
I have nothing

to fight with.
The stove cools, armed

and willing are two
things, I hear you say.

Can you see me
from the sky?

Will the schoolhouse
sigh as it gives in?

The children bear
weaponry. I am

madly. Hard crumb
in my windpipe all day.

Lament for the Living

where there is silence   there is nothing
I can say   to replace   what the water has entered
and ruined   what the rain wipes away

where there was a town   there is fire
there is nothing

I can say   a black mold blooms
a hollowing
a blue flame licks its prey

where there is a city
or say   there is no city

with its lines of sky
where there is nothing   say the moon
asserts itself   between the clouds

where the darkness is   a curtain and the stars
have this secret

Matter in Retreat

The stars drift
away from one another

tonight as every moment you
& I breathing so thoughtless a living

we make as we are made to
as I make another promise

to myself to try to mean more
to you to call out across

a great distance but I am not
loud enough I suspect I have not

enough protest in me
the arc of my throat awaits

a tenderness or a brutality
& what are we

to one another but a means
to a meaning we haven't yet

discovered two points of light
on the inky dark

sky two paper boats
on a black lake floating further

away every day I awake
I roll over I hide my head

we get smaller our living it's pathetic
I mean it makes you sad

Little Children, My Apologies

I was considering the sea: all the colors
it has taught me, how water is at once
both life and deadly.
In my comfortable way, I come to learn, the dangers
are many and oblique:
the microwave will kill me, this plastic bottle, this air,
this meat, my debit card and its hidden fees. I'm telling you,
I have no power here. I'm just a dummy swaddled
in worry and want, tethered
by two small rooms, a few small thoughts.
You know how the body is
a fragile thing. Phosphorus gleams, clings
to your skin and won't let go,
and my great sleep spreads out into the day
like milk spilled on the cold tile floor.
I am thinking of you. The dark is chilly,
framed by the window. Outside
they are constructing another tower.
A high-rise, this time. The progress is quick.
The walls are bones. One naked bulb glows
in each half-built home.

Forbearance

I owe everything money but all I have
is nightmares.

(Jawbone vise, stiff neck, chewed cheek.)

I come to and nothing.

(*Good morning, good morning, nothing.*)

In other words, I bring the spirits back
and put them away.

Or, rather, I lied. I meant to say, I owe you
everything, money, but all I have

is this love, this empty
cupboard, this closet full of ugly
things.

I tell you, you are wrong
about me, as I am wrong
about what all these dreams mean.

I, like everything else, am a carcinogen.
My limbs complain.
(*I come to nothing, I tell you.*)

I put my little light out.

I meant to say, I lied. I have this roof
to be under, this home
I eat myself out of with every meal.

I come to and put my ugly things away. In other words,

(*good morning, love*)

the bed is a hilly landscape, perfect with you in it.

(The ceiling opens, my little light shines.)

We arrange our dreams against the wind.

Instructions for the Forest

Never mind what lies beyond
the canopy. The city

is a dream. The sound of traffic isn't
traffic, but a swift wind

through the leaves.
Before the city,

there were these woods,
this black oak tree,

there were armies in an uproar
over whose land this would be.

It turns out, this land was made
for the living

and the dying
of natural things. Never mind

the city. On the forest floor
what rots tomorrow feeds

what's taking root today.
We are the understory:

reaching for a tear in the tarp
that masks the sky.

Forget the fence
and the fire hydrant,

what work's left to be done.
It turns out, this life

is a dream, built on a rock
set afloat on an infinite sea.

Somewhere Else

Two stray dogs sleep on the step,
Someone paints
Their hot roof blue, hangs
Eager yellow curtains.

In the meantime, America,
Limp with worry, bought out,
Fraying under God and needing
To be lowered to the ground and lit up.

Across town the commodity has arrived
In several colors, keeping your face
Lukewarm, keeping you in business,
Collecting dust.

What could possess you now but the barbed wire
And the Exit sign, on fire for a reason:
Someone waits behind a wood door, a stone floor,
Two dogs, heads on their paws, ready.

Symptoms of Home

1

When the mill shut down I was heavy as water.
We all went to work screwing in lightbulbs, changing
positions in a white box and were afraid.

I'd wait on doorsteps after, licking my halogen wounds,
hoping to be home, sweet again. These days
I was shrink-wrapped unsound, following

you as if you were the moon I set my clock by, pleading
to be put back or socketed stiff to the dry wall. This is how
we wept in the old country: knees together.

2

In the drought days the walls drip wanting and we watch
out the windows for a promising gray. It goes on like this.
Up the road a ways an old man tells stories of a great wave.

Dust takes to the air at a glance. We rattle it with our breath
and wait to sneeze and wait. Green shrinks to the ground.
It goes on like this.

3

Take calm to your homeland — the storm passed
this way. The trees show it. The lights went out that day
and stayed out. Candles pooled

and stilled. Children cried for milk, fathers
took to the dark and stayed out. The three stars you knew
lost in new company. We'd never met

a black like this. The absent skyline, the howl
of a dog made strange. Oh, the gall of the ghosts
in our wake. The gall of them.

Genealogy

I was born in a forest.
I don't know my name.
I was born on a mountain but changed
my mind. I was born
in the desert. All my people died
in the fire and left me
with the gods. They called me dust.
How it burned me. I come from the sea,
I believe. I come from beryl,
aquamarine. All my people
rode their horses off
the edge of the world and left me
on your doorstep. They called me
sorrow. I don't know my name.
I come from wartime. How it burned me.
I was born aflame, I believe. A sun
so intentional. A sun in repose, a sun
in continuous sunset, sinking into the ground.

The Free World

I bind my old   grievances
    to a helium balloon.   A long memory,

I have been warned,
    is a curse.   Everywhere I go,   someone

has something   they must say   about you.
    Nobody knows   who we are.   Wouldn't you say,

nobody   agonizes like we do.
    Elsewhere

is a promise   and a threat.
    I have been proscribed

compassion   of the wrong sort, and so
    I am alone.   I am

invisible within you.   Seeking companionship
    I spend   my afternoons   before the windows

of pet shops and   strangers, trying
    to decide.   After all, I was told

I could have everything.
    I thought   this was meant to be

a romance: I was delivered here
    in order to love you.

I was delivered here
    and ordered

to love you. If   we could be friends.
     I wore this new   dress for you.

Dry Harbour

for John Dudley Rankine, 1916–2010

At the shore, the water is rush
    and retreat, taking my footprints
with it, a quiet delete.

    What's buried here won't stay
in the ground. Now you are gone,
    I make you again

and again: you are the boy
    in the harbour
on another hot day,

    you are the boy watching
the horses leap over your head
    to cool themselves

in the harbour, you are
    the man daydreaming
the horses leap into the harbour,

    their ripple and gleam.
I've come to understand
    we are accident

and disease: a door
    left open, a gust, a weed. A ship
docked in the wrong harbour, a pandemic

    liquidation through the hills,
the cane fields, and then
    there was you, and then

there was me, with no land but this
mouth, and the dead
who can't speak —

oh, people of the earth,
how easily they slip
back into it. How tired I am

of these bodies
in the water, of what's lost
that can't come back.

The ocean spills
and swallows
and remains steadfast.

Syzygy

I was told tonight   the moon
         would be impossible   but I am too drunk
                  my eyes toward the sky   I feel

I would come loose   from the earth
         a short flight   I believe
                  I've bitten off more than can be held

at bay   in which case it helps
         to think collectively
                  however unlikely   here we are

rooting for the doomed
         gazelle   or we are the gazelle
                  we are the lion

or the birds of prey   the land-
         locked boy daydreaming
                  an expanse of blue

the earth curves
         we mark the dates and keep
                  waking up   turning the clock

forward and back   in the quiet
         we step quietly
                  in the audience   we stand

and demand more   we clap our hands
         in captivity   we carve our name
                  into the floor

We

have been the buyer, the bought
    the boy's blood in the dirt

have been the woman in winter
    the knife of her hunger

have been the knife at her throat

have ravaged and burned, been burned

have been the rope that hangs
    the hands that bind the hands, that set the flame

have been a land cleared by the flame
    a land lit by the moon
    a sky cleared by lit homes

have been a man reduced
    to a body, a body to bones

have emboldened, been made bold

have been uplifted, held
    under, mourned, been mourned

have been a tale told
    and untold

have been a language lost
    owning nothing of ourselves

have been a love that dims
        the line drawn between us to remind

have deceived, been taken in

have been destroyed
have been beginning

have been discovery, a new fruit
        growing ripe within our skins

Notes

Incorrect Merciful Impulses
The title of this collection comes from a line in Jenny Holzer's series of text-based art pieces, *Inflammatory Essays*.

"On the Motion of Animals"
"The movements of animals may be compared with those of automatic puppets, which are set going on the occasion of a tiny movement; the levers are released, and strike the twisted strings against one another" (Aristotle, *On the Motion of Animals*).

"The Problem of Death within Life"
The title is lifted from Martha Nussbaum's essay "Compassion and Terror," where she discusses the philosophy of Marcus Aurelius, "in which we respect all human beings and view all as our partners in a common project whose terms don't seem to matter very much, thus rendering the whole point of living in the world increasingly unclear. And this means something like a death within life. For only in a condition close to death, in effect, is moral rectitude possible."

"The Increasing Frequency of Black Swans"
The term Black Swan refers to Nassim Nicholas Taleb's theory of Black Swan events, which he characterizes as events of rarity and extreme impact. "A small number of Black Swans explain almost everything in our world, from the success of ideas and religions, to the dynamics of historical events, to elements of our own personal lives" (Taleb, *The Black Swan: The Impact of the Highly Improbable*).

"Symptoms of Doctrine"
"I have been burdened with glorious purpose" is a line of dialogue from the 2012 film *The Avengers*.

"Possession"
"I love the great despisers, because they are the great adorers, and arrows of longing for the other shore" (Friedrich Nietzsche, *Thus Spake Zarathustra: A Book for All and None*).

"Dry Harbour"
This is the name Christopher Columbus gave the bay where it is believed his ships first landed in Jamaica. It has since been renamed Discovery Bay.

About the Author

Camille Rankine is the author of the chapbook *Slow Dance with Trip Wire,* selected by Cornelius Eady for the Poetry Society of America's 2010 New York Chapbook Fellowship. She is the recipient of a 2010 "Discovery"/ Boston Review Poetry Prize and a MacDowell Colony Fellowship, and her poetry has appeared in *Boston Review, Denver Quarterly, A Public Space, Tin House,* and elsewhere. Assistant director of the MFA Program in Creative Writing at Manhattanville College, Rankine lives in New York City.

Lannan Literary Selections

For two decades Lannan Foundation has supported the publication
and distribution of exceptional literary works. Copper Canyon Press
gratefully acknowledges their support.

LANNAN LITERARY SELECTIONS 2015

Michael Dickman, *Green Migraine*

Deborah Landau, *The Uses of the Body*

Camille Rankine, *Incorrect Merciful Impulses*

Richard Siken, *War of the Foxes*

Frank Stanford, *What About This: Collected Poems of Frank Stanford*

RECENT LANNAN LITERARY SELECTIONS FROM COPPER CANYON PRESS

James Arthur, *Charms Against Lightning*

Mark Bibbins, *They Don't Kill You Because They're Hungry,
They Kill You Because They're Full*

Malachi Black, *Storm Toward Morning*

Marianne Boruch, *Cadaver, Speak*

Jericho Brown, *The New Testament*

Olena Kalytiak Davis, *The Poem She Didn't Write and Other Poems*

Natalie Diaz, *When My Brother Was an Aztec*

Matthew Dickman and Michael Dickman, *50 American Plays*

Kerry James Evans, *Bangalore*

Tung-Hui Hu, *Greenhouses, Lighthouses*

Deborah Landau, *The Last Usable Hour*

Sarah Lindsay, *Debt to the Bone-Eating Snotflower*

Michael McGriff, *Home Burial*

Valzhyna Mort, *Collected Body*

Lisa Olstein, *Little Stranger*

Roger Reeves, *King Me*

Ed Skoog, *Rough Day*

For a complete list of Lannan Literary Selections from
Copper Canyon Press, please visit Partners on our website:
www.coppercanyonpress.org

Poetry is vital to language and living. Since 1972, Copper Canyon Press has published extraordinary poetry from around the world to engage the imaginations and intellects of readers, writers, booksellers, librarians, teachers, students, and donors.

WE ARE GRATEFUL FOR THE MAJOR SUPPORT PROVIDED BY:

THE PAUL G. ALLEN FAMILY FOUNDATION

CULTURE

Lannan

OFFICE OF ARTS & CULTURE
SEATTLE

Anonymous

John Branch

Diana Broze

Beroz Ferrell & The Point, LLC

Janet and Les Cox

Mimi Gardner Gates

Linda Gerrard and Walter Parsons

Gull Industries, Inc.
    on behalf of William and
    Ruth True

Mark Hamilton and Suzie Rapp

Carolyn and Robert Hedin

Steven Myron Holl

Lakeside Industries, Inc.
    on behalf of Jeanne Marie Lee

Maureen Lee and Mark Busto

Brice Marden

Ellie Mathews and Carl Youngmann
    as The North Press

H. Stewart Parker

Penny and Jerry Peabody

John Phillips and Anne O'Donnell

Joseph C. Roberts

Cynthia Lovelace Sears and
    Frank Buxton

The Seattle Foundation

Kim and Jeff Seely

David and Catherine Eaton Skinner

Dan Waggoner

C.D. Wright and Forrest Gander

Charles and Barbara Wright

The dedicated interns and faithful volunteers of Copper Canyon Press

TO LEARN MORE ABOUT UNDERWRITING COPPER CANYON PRESS TITLES, PLEASE CALL 360-385-4925 EXT. 103

The Chinese character for poetry is made up of two parts: "word" and "temple." It also serves as pressmark for Copper Canyon Press.

The text is set in Baskerville 10, František Štorm's digital reworking of the eighteenth-century English type of John Baskerville. Titles are set in Adrian Frutiger's Avenir. Book design and composition by VJB/Scribe. Printed on archival-quality paper.